About The Author

Thank you for allowing me to share some of my thoughts and ideas with you. I'm a husband, Father and entrepreneur. I honor God, the Creator as my source of wisdom and power. Since I started my fitness career, after my Marine Corps career was complete in 2003, I have had the pleasure of traveling all over and meeting Trainers of numerous facets and interesting people from all walks of life. Through developing relationships, both personal and business, I have learned that selflessness is the key to true success. Through selflessness you are able to draw people to you more effectively and keep them positively intrigued longer.

Having trained hundreds of people with every kind of background and ambition you can imagine, my desire is to help others better themselves while I do the same in the process for myself.

Copyright © 2014 by Robert W. Campbell II

Case# 1-1292030571

All Rights Reserved. This book, or parts thereof, may not be reproduced in any form without permission.

Published simultaneously in Europe, Canada, Asia and Great Britain

Library of Congress Cataloging-in-Publication Data

Campbell, Robert W. II

Personal Training: Master The Art/Robert W. Campbell II

ISBN-13: 978-0615996776

Printed in the United States of America

www.CoachRobCam.com

Master The Art of Personal Training

Contents

About the Author 1
Introduction 6
Why Are You Here? 10
Who Cares? 13
As Seen Everywhere 17
Peer-To-Peer 22
It's Business, Sometimes Personal 25
Remember Me? 30
How Do I Look 33
The Chicken Or The Egg? 38
The Value And The Cost 40
Under The Table, Beneath The Ethics .44
Book Head 48
The Wall 51
What Do You know About Me? 54
Give It To Me Straight 58
The Middle Man 61
See You At 5 64
Do It, Do It, Do It 67

Do I have To? 70
0 to 100 72
One Size Fits All. No It Doesn't 75
Here We Go Again 79
The More The Merrier 82
So How Are Things Going? 85
Conclusion 88

Introduction

Serving an eight-year tour in the Marine Corp and then transitioning back into the civilian world is not easy. However countless people go through this transition each and every day. In 2001, a month after the terrorist attack of 9-11, it was my turn. Having friends previously transition and earning lots of money in sales industries, I found that to be a very attractive transitional career for me as well. So under the advice of one of those friends, I joined an insurance agency, got licensed and indeed made a lot of money. However, amidst all the rewards I received, there was still a void deep in my soul that needed fulfillment.

The whole sales career thing took me into other fields where I tested my skills with different products and services to see which would lead me to the promised land of financial freedom, prosperity and an early retirement, all to no avail. Fortunately a friend of mine who I worked with in the car sales business, which I hated by the way, got a job with a local franchise of a national gym chain.

He was so excited that I was excited for him. He turned in his one-day resignation, and my response was "can I come too?" I did, and that's where everything started to change.

My first job as a gym membership sales consultant led me into personal training, club management and eventually, club ownership. Of all that I've done, personal training is by far the most invigorating to this day.

You will notice in this book, that I offer no cookie cutter workouts, recipes or anything in the way of kinesiology. This is not an exercise book. It's not a nutrition book. This book has a different intention and is different in some ways to all who read it. As you read, you will understand exactly what it is for yourself. My only hope is that you take the time to read it with a sheer desire to become the greatest Personal Trainer or Coach you can possibly be.

I spend each day of my life hoping to make a lasting and beneficial impact on someone's life before lying down to sleep another night. This should be your mindset as well. You are a Motivator. Get out there and motivate.

"The most absolute way to not succeed is to not try at all."
- Robert W. Campbell II

Why are you here?

With millions of career choices in the world, we all have options as to what we want to wake up and invest our time into each day. Yet becoming a Personal Trainer is a choice that so many of us have made.

With anything in life, you want to have a good reason to do something, especially if it will take up most of your time, some of your money and will continue to do so for years to come. Sometimes people decide to go into a career field to later find that they are not really made for it. I have seen this happen countless times through the years.

I have met many Personal Trainers who were new to the field and had a big vision for how they were going to make a big splash in the industry, only to get discouraged shortly after. This is unfortunate, not only for the Trainer, but also their unassuming clients and their employers.

The problem with these Trainers is that they were not passionate enough about creating a legacy of success and stellar service. Helping people live a better life has to be your number one passion in this industry or you will be mediocre at best as a

Trainer. Sure, a money hungry hustler can do well with the right clientele, but usually this type will fall into unethical practices, get found out and move onto the next money chasing hustle.

Hopefully, as you read this book, it will either confirm your passion for helping others achieve, or confirm the fact that you are in this field for the wrong reasons. Personal Trainers can make a lot of money, but that should be the byproduct of a focused passion, attention to detail and dedication to our cause.

"Of course motivation is not permanent. But then, neither is bathing; but it is something you should do on a regular basis."
- *Zig Ziglar*

Who Cares?

Why should anyone care that you exist or much less, what you know or can do? The truth is, everyone on earth can benefit from having his or her very own Personal Trainer. Show me a professional athlete that doesn't have at least one trainer and at least one coach. I'll give you as much time as you need to come back and tell me you didn't find any.

You are a very important piece of the puzzle to help the world live its best life. If you didn't know that, now you do. Keep that in mind, but also remember that the majority of the world doesn't care that you exist and aren't looking for your help. You think you're awesome, but most of them don't think of you at all. It's your job to make yourself noticeable, marketable, approachable and prepared for whomever does approach you for assistance. For every 10 people who couldn't care less about you, there is one who would be delighted to have you in their corner. Be prepared at all times to accommodate that one. It's a numbers game. The more people you meet, the more opportunities you will have. Don't fret over the ones you don't attract. Simply keep yourself visible and productive to attract more of the ones who will inquire of your expertise.

I have to point out one of my biggest pet peeves here. You have the greatest opportunity to attract people who will find you necessary by doing one very simple thing. That one thing is to be seen in action. When people can see a product or service in action producing something fascinating, they can more easily visualize themselves benefiting from it also. If you have plenty of clientele, this is easy because you will be out on the floor being seen anyway. For those of you who are new to the industry and have not built your book yet, I'm going to share with you an extremely easy way to pull this off. The pet peeve I was talking about is that young Trainers usually feel entitled and expect people to flock to them because they are young, in shape and are wearing a "TRAINER" shirt. In your dreams "Mr. Awesome". These Trainers refuse to offer anything for free because their egos have convinced them that they are a hot commodity and people are supposed to be pushing and shoving to get a spot on their appointment book. The reality is just as I stated above. You have to put in work because most people DO NOT care whom the guy in the Trainer shirt is. So fix your attitude and get to work.

Here is what you need to do. It works miraculously. I've coached many Trainers in this method and all the ones who humbled themselves to do it properly are all very successfully today. The ones who didn't are still gym hopping and blaming other people and the economy for their failure.

My method is to give some of your time for free. Yes, for free. Here is how it works. Gather a couple of people who need your services and sign them to a pro-bono agreement. You will train them in exchange for their testimonials. Do a fantastic job and the testimonials will serve you well. The other amazingly sweet part of this arrangement is that these free clients get you on the floor, which creates the illusion that you, as a new Trainer have already started to fill your client book. In an onlooker's mind, you must be pretty good to have done this. Do a great job on the floor for the entire world to see, and you will most definitely have other gym members approaching you to ask how they can get an appointment with you.

"All great achievements require time."
- *Maya Angelou*

As Seen Everywhere

Making yourself known, highly visible and accessible is essential to your success. If people know you exist, what you can do for them and how they can reach you, you greatly increase your potential for obtaining new clientele.

There are many ways to increase your visibility. Some will require a small financial investment, while there are plenty of free options. Using technology is a must in modern business. That's if you want to maximize your reach and visibility. Start with free methods of social networking. Opening dedicated fitness based accounts on Facebook, Twitter and like networks is easy and will provide lots of opportunity to attract people to you. Use these to build your audience and promote yourself by offering weekly fitness and health tips, short educational videos and blog posts.

Email is also important to use for business communication. If you launch a website, open an email account to match the site. Your web-hosting package should have this as a bonus or an add-on. If you work for someone else's company, ask to be issued a company email.

This greatly increases your credibility over having a basic free email account with a public provider.

Another credibility building, area saturation method is press releases. Getting into the local newspaper and appearing on the local news channel is a surefire way to boost your reputation and get your appointment book filled. The best part about this method is lots of newspapers will interview you and print your bio for free as a new business in their area, so it's essential that you reach out to them in the beginning stages of establishing yourself. You may even be so fortunate as to gain a consistent column in the newspaper, offering expert tips relevant to your field.

One other thing that has worked very well for me is making public appearances at local events and programs. Speaking at local school career day events greatly increased my credibility in the community. Volunteering at community building events is also a great way to build your circle of associates and get face time with potential clients in your neighborhood. As weird as it may seem, teaming up with other Trainers to do these kinds of things is a very smart idea. This would be a display of your professionalism, sincere desire for the greater good of your community and to gain allies in your field.

Finally, you will need to saturate your area with promotional items to create you and your company a recognizable name in your area. This is where fliers, door hangers and other print resources come in. Get as much of these out in the public as possible. Building networking relationships with local businesses is the key to making this work most efficiently with less work and cost. Using cross-promotions is a great way of achievement this. Team up with another business that has a large reach and have them help you distribute your materials. You may want to offer them something for helping you, like a discount on training for the key person, or a free membership to your facility. One of my favorite relationships is one I have with local nutrition stores. My friends in these establishments simply place my fliers and promotional postcards in their customer's bags. I know it works, because the customers bring them in to redeem the offer I have on them.

Use this method with numerous businesses and watch your popularity soar in no time. Even if your promo items don't translate to immediate sales, they do their job of getting your name out into the public.

"Talent is a wonderful thing, but it won't carry a quitter."
- Stephen King, *Duma Key*

Peer To Peer

Iron Sharpens iron. Learn from one another. A cocky arrogant "I already know that" attitude will bury you. Any smart businessperson knows the value of networking and making allies amongst peers. If a person likes you just a little bit, it's better than them totally not liking you.

When you form an alliance with your peers, it opens up tremendous opportunity to share ideas and strengthen your team as a whole. The most successful Trainers in our industry, when you talk to them, they typically endorse other Trainers. What? Yes, it's true. I have worked my many top level and celebrity Trainers and each of them has at some point mentioned that another Trainer inspired them in some way or they had recently enjoyed working with another Trainer on a collaborative project. This is the way our industry should work. We should be able to refer clientele to one another and enhance our overall reputation by being confident in our peers and ourselves.

In many small gyms across America, the peer-to-peer method of growth and success has been abandoned and the "do me" and "get mine" method is prevalent.

This is the way of the foolish. The wise seek to make allies as opposed to making enemies. Let's all adopt a wise method of life and of business.

"Your talent determines what you can do. Your motivation determines how much you are willing to do. Your attitude determines how well you do it."
- *Lou Holtz*

It's business, sometimes personal

Personal training is a business. It's as simple as that. If you treat it like a hobby, you will not only eliminate yourself from the industry quickly, you also contribute to damaging the image of the industry as a whole by minimizing what we do in your service recipient's eyes. Yes, giving yourself away too much causes people to get a distorted view of the value of Personal Trainer. It's no different than anything else. If a shoe company started off their shoes for $5 a pair for the first two years, it would be almost impossible for them to get $200 for the same pair of shoes in the following year. This idea applies to all service and merchandise industries, including ours. From time to time you may bend the rules on this, but be very sparing and decisive about it.

You will at times take a personal stake in certain people i.e. your close family members and best friends. Be sure to not overextend yourself in these circumstances. An occasional fitness or nutrition tip is fine, but you should never get so extended into giving away your services to friends and family that you negatively affect your earning potential and/or let this use up so much of your time that you have less time to devote to existing paying clients.

Charge what you're worth! One of the biggest mistakes good Trainers make is underselling themselves. When you enter the industry you put yourself through several preparatory steps before you take on clients. You study, get certified, invest in proper work attire, buy insurance and many other things before you even get started in the field. Although this, in the beginning is preparatory, it's actually what you will continue to do throughout your career. You have to continue your education, be presentable and in great shape and market yourself amongst other things.

All of this takes money. To pay for these things, you will be reinvesting the profit you are making from your work. This means you will need to make enough to support your career necessities and then enough to support your standard of living. The best way to do this is to make you and your services worth a premium service rate. Premium service rates are high only in the eyes of those you don't give premium results to. In other words, if you are ensuring your clients succeed and doing it in a way they couldn't have done on their own, you can easily justify charging premium rate.

The best part is that the client will know it and will have no problem paying it. Intelligent people understand that the best comes at a price. Which brings me to my next point.

Don't waste your time with people who don't want to pay what you're worth. Notice I said, "don't want to". You may at some point find yourself being told that your rates are ridiculous or that someone else at some other place charges far less among other insults. If you can overcome it and still gain that person as a client, do so. If not, disregard it and move on. These people are not the same as the ones who can't afford to pay you. At times you will encounter those who can't afford to pay premium rate. Offer them a slight reduction at your discretion, but be wise about this. As discussed earlier, you don't want to overextend yourself in these circumstances and wind up not making enough money to sustain your quality of life and your business

Another important conversation under this same subject is fraternization.

Don't do it! Business is business. Keep it that way. Trainers are in a sense, Counselors.

From time to time clients will lean on you for advice, reassurance and sympathy about things in their personal lives. Let your counsel be limited and related to the business relationship between you. Giving relationship advice is a no-no and could easily come back to bite you hard. When clients try to include you in these things, simply say, "that's a bit out of my line of expertise" and follow that with "but, I'm here to help you make *this* part of your life an enjoyable success." Ensure your client that the exercise sessions should be used as a stress relief outlet and they should try to leave all negative thoughts outside of this time.

Understanding the above, you should easily be able to understand that making sexual advances toward your clients; using obscene language and engaging in distracting conversation are all unacceptable for a professional Trainer. All of these can lead down a part of career suicide and you did not start your career to have it all fall apart, especially for doing something you could have opted not to.

"Get comfortable with being uncomfortable!"
- *Jillian Michaels*

Remember me?

In everyday life we meet new people all the time. Every day provides new opportunities to build your clientele base and your reputation in the community. To say "never waste an opportunity" would be too vague. I prefer to say that you should never waste an opportunity you have already embarked on. In other words, take full advantage of every new encounter you have with a potential client or person who can spread the word about you. There are several ways to do this.

Always get the person's name and use it frequently in conversation so they remember you as a person who pays attention. Also you will want to be sure they know your name. To do this, make interesting conversation rather than a bland "hi my name is" and "goodbye, call me". Finding out interesting things about them and showing a dedicated interest in them and their life is a surefire way to leave a great impression. In this approach, you can key on similar interests or contrasting circumstances to build a more solid connection.

To add a layer of strength to this meet, leave them with an attractive custom business card, preferably with your name, face, contact and an offer that will draw them to contact you.

If you are really good, you will be able to gather their contact info. This way you can program them into your appointments with a reminder to follow up with them. Do your follow up in timed increments that will show a professional concern and consistency that will keep them interested in and remembering you.

To go a bit further into the impressive professional realm, on your first follow up call, gather the potential client's birthday and email address. This will allow you to extend best wishes and special offers to them on their birthday and other holidays and special occasions.

"The reason fat men are good natured is they can neither fight nor run."
- *Theodore Roosevelt*

How do I look?

Look the part! Trainers have no business being out of shape. If you are, you should have no business. You don't deserve to be in business if you can't at least practice what you preach. However, there are exceptions to this standard. Pregnancy of course would be an exception. Another would be a Trainer who has gotten certified during the process of reaching for his or her own fitness goals. This would be someone who was on a personal fitness regimen, made progresses and got so excited that they themselves wanted to motivate others. In either situation, it's a best practice to let your personal situation be made public knowledge. We have to remember that perception is everything. If potential clients know your situation, it will hinder them from perceiving that you are simply an out of shape hypocrite, rather, seeing you as motivating others while handling your own physical challenges may in fact boost your credibility with them.

Moving on, there are other areas we need to be extremely attentive to. Hygiene is one of them. No one wants to be in the presence of someone with poor hygiene, especially someone they expect to promote a healthy lifestyle, like a Personal Trainer.

With that said, keep your breathe fresh, your body clean and your grooming sharp. If you have a meal, freshen up immediately after. Smart Trainers are well organized and stay prepared for anything. Packing a hygiene kit in your gym bag is the way to go.

Apparel is also important. I personally recommend wearing apparel that displays your company logo, whether you are independent or working with another firm. In addition, your apparel should be clean, neat and in a size that is appropriate for your body. There are varying opinions on what is appropriate fitness apparel. I personally feel that when you are in a leadership position, you should be wise to dress in a way that is non-offensive and non-intimidating to your clients and potential clients. Remember you are not working out, you are coaching others and they see you as a mentor. With that in mind, showing less skin and curves may be better since we know that many who are struggling with their image are already easily intimidated. Also we don't want to appear to be deliberately enticing clients or onlookers.

Finally, we get to what may be the most important thing about image.

The way you carry yourself and the vibes you give off could make or break your career and reputation.

As a novice Trainer, I was lousy with sales pitches, but I was a master of sales pitches at the same time. How can that be? Well, it turns out that I was never sold on the old school hard core back-a-cat-in-the-corner sales tactics I was taught in the sales training I received from the big chain gym I was first employed by. However, I was blessed with all the attributes I needed to sell as much PT as I needed to…ever. Once I branched out on my own, I was able to find my true skills and use them as freely as I wanted. Those skills had everything to do with how I looked, not so much what I said.

Here is my method. Use body language that shows a sincere interest in what your clients are saying. Even if they are a rambler, be a great listener, take lots of notes and stay tuned in. When you walk, walk with confidence, not arrogance, confidence. Confidence attracts people who both have equal confidence and also those who have a serious lack of confidence but want to change that. Smile a lot, and I mean a lot. Being approachable and appearing that way is extremely important.

This would include the way you train in your off time.

You are always on display and you have to remember that people are constantly evaluating you. If your appearance, demeanor or attitude intimidates people, they may not approach you to inquire about your services.

"Always make a total effort, even when the odds are against you."
- *Arnold Palmer*

The chicken or the egg?

What should happen first, the payment or the training? Get paid up front! Paying clients are loyal clients. They have made the financial commitment and now its time for you to prove to them they made a worthy investment.

Keeping proper financial records is a must. Have a reliable method of record keeping. If you don't have one that works, get one. You should always reserve your client's sessions in paid blocks that you simplify redeem as you go. If no payment has been received, no blocks can be reserved. I do this in a club management software. The software simplifies it because it will not allow me to book sessions on a client that has no money applied in the system. Therefore I have no chance of accidentally rendering session to a client that has no sessions left, which many disorganized Trainers have admitted to doing. Um, oh yeah, I've done it too. Shame on us.

There are two exceptions to the rule. Exception #1 is if you have a loyal client who performs well, always pays on time and asks to pay you on a date slightly beyond their last prepaid session.

If you allow this, you absolute must make it clear that it is an exception, not to be made frequently. You also have to be sure to keep accurate records to document this occurrence so you don't lose track. Once again, both you and your client must understand that this cannot be an ongoing trend.

Exception #2 would be a brand new client that you didn't intend on meeting today and they didn't intend on meeting you. For instance, you met someone in the gym today, had a conversation and decided to go ahead and do an assessment. Upon completing the assessment you offer a free starter session and consequently sign him or her to a PT agreement. Sure give some of your time and show them your skills, but have the intension to convert them into your client.

"Without self-discipline, success is impossible, period."
- *Lou Holtz*

The value and the cost

You're worth every penny you charge for your services. Well, are you?

Trainers are on the preventive side of the healthcare system. We try to reduce the number of visits people need to make to the doctor's office, thus saving them medical expenses, gas, time and loss of work hours. This in itself creates a tremendous value to the service we provide given the client understands this. As a professional, it's part of your job to make sure they do.

Another thing your potential clients need to understand is that the Personal Trainer is capable of reducing stress. Here is how. Figuring out how much exercise to do, what exercise to do at what increment and so on, is extremely stressful. This is especially true when the person has no clue if the program they choose is the one that will work for them. What's even more frustrating is when they find out that it didn't work. This is the point where most people get frustrated enough to quit. All of these are moments when stress sets in and can even lead to depression. Depression will put them right back in the situation we tried to rescue them from, back in the doctor's office.

What I'm saying here is that it's more than the sale, and what we sell is far more than a superficial fad product. You have the ability to enhance a person's quality-of-life and help them live longer and stronger. That is priceless. As a trainer if you don't understand that, you have completely missed the main reason any of us should be in this industry. We are here for the benefit of others and what we provide as a service is well worth what we ask for in compensation.

"If you aren't going all the way, why go at all?"
- *Joe Namath*

Under the table, Beneath The Ethics

Business ethics is always a #1 priority no matter what industry you are in. Reliability and integrity are superior attributes that everyone must possess to most effectively serve others. With that being said, I would like to point out an ongoing problem in our industry that has destroyed many relationships and tarnished careers of promising Trainers.

Everyone wants to earn as much as possible when compensation is part of the deal. Good ethics would have you to handle business in a manner that is honorable to the agreement you have made with the other parties of the agreement, whether it's a client or a fitness facility. In my years of working in and out of fitness facilities, I have periodically experienced Trainers break the code of ethics and honor to increase their personal revenue. There is one method in particular that troubles me. I'll explain in detail what the problem is, how it starts and what must be done to remedy it.

Some fitness facilities hire Trainers on a commission-only pay method. In this system the Trainer gets paid a percentage of the money they collect for personal training services they render to clients they train within that facility. This can be relevant to members of the facility or clients who come to the facility for personal training only. This system is usually set to pay the Trainer a higher commission considering they don't get paid a salary or hourly rate. For Trainers who are good at converting prospective clients into actual clients, this is the ideal format to work under and many do very well. I myself have favored this system since the day I found out I had become pretty good at converting.

Here is where things go terribly wrong. Sometimes there are Trainers who forget their commitment to ethics and a high level of service. When this happens they find themselves doing business in a way to only benefit them instead of honoring their agreement with the client and facility. In an effort to increase personal wealth, there are sometimes Trainers who will ask a client to pay them "under the table". This allows the Trainer to cut the facility out of the revenue percentage that the facility should rightfully collect.

This is stealing, fraud and just plain wrong. What's worse is that in doing this, the Trainer has coerced the unsuspecting client into participating in this larceny scheme. This is wrong on many levels and needs to be stopped. I personally witnessed a very good self-starter Trainer ruin his career and reputation by doing unethical business. Unfortunately, it also hurts the image of Trainers in general for a short time. It makes people a bit skeptical of us all.

How do we get rid of the problem? There is only one way. Each of us has to have our own internal integrity and exercise proper ethics. Things tend to come out in the wash so to speak. It's only a matter of time before a member of our ranks who doesn't belong, will be weeded out. Each and every Trainer has to evaluate him or herself and make sure they have what it takes to build a successful and honorable career in this industry. Those of us who have what it takes tend to stick around for a long time. We know how to negotiate our compensation and we know how to earn what we are worth within the code of ethics.

"Your biggest opponent isn't the other guy. It's human nature."
- *Bobby Knight*

Book Head

Know your stuff! All of us want to be thought of as knowledgeable. This is why we study and practice our art. Our learning should not be for the moment or just to handle the situation of the day. We should always study to learn and retain. I've known eager Trainers coming into the industry who have crammed for a certification exam only to lose most of the learned knowledge a short time after. Sure, cramming can probably get you through a testing phase, but it won't do you or your clients any good if you don't remember anything when it's time for action.

The remedy to this dilemma is to get your head back in the books. Study your basic knowledge on kinesiology, Anatomy and the industry in general. Every Trainer should understand the human body, how it works and what is best for its performance and maintenance. Sometimes you will get into a rhythm of doing the same thing every day, only using a small portion of your knowledge. Reviewing past studies is always recommended to keep your mind sharp and to refresh your thinking.

Trainers should also stay well informed on the ever changing fitness industry and the medical world. Treatment and avoidance of injuries and diseases has constant new developments, including new medicines you may encounter in your client's prescription list. This research would also include the supplement industry. New nutrition and sports supplements arrive on the market almost daily. If it could land in the hands if your clients, you should know its out there. We need to stay in tune with what's happening in the world that affects us both directly and indirectly.

"There are only two options regarding commitment. You're either IN or you're OUT. There is no such thing as life in-between."
- *Pat Riley*

The Wall

Passionate Trainers often throw themselves head first into their work. They want to create a full book of clientele and make the money they deserve in the process. They promote themselves all over town and they hate to turn anyone away. Passionate Trainers operate this way and it's the way you should think initially. As a beginner you should gain as much experience as you can to develop yourself, but you will have to manage your commitments and strategize well to prevent burnout.

Often times, Personal Trainers attract new clients with immensely varied scheduling availability. This can lead to a wide spread daily calendar due to having to place clients in timeslots they can commit to. One of the easiest ways to burn yourself out is to spread sessions out sporadically all throughout the day, everyday. Another almost counterproductive situation some Trainers get into is reducing the cost for long time loyal clients and then giving that same client more sessions. What you've done is occupy more of your schedule for less money.

The worst part is that in the slots where you've extended your existing "VIP" rate client, you will most certainly meet lots of people who would like sessions during those same time slots and gladly pay full rate. Oops! Now look what you've done.

"Never let your head hang down. Never give up and sit down and grieve. Find another way."
- *Satchel Paige*

What do you know about me?

The first thing any Trainer needs to do when taking on a potential client is to have an in-depth professional conversation with them. Your client has lots of questions they really want answered and you have just as many for them. The initial meet & greet will allow for almost all of the preliminary questions on both sides to be addressed.

Getting to know your client is imperative to how engaged they will be in this new undertaking and also to how much you gather to be able to plan their programming wisely. There is no way you can create a custom program for someone you know nothing about.

The physical activity readiness questionnaire (PAR-Q) will cover a portion of what you need to know about your new client's medical status. This form is mandatory to complete and needs to be done prior to instructing your client to perform any physical tasks.

Along with the PAR-Q, it's wise to add some additional questions to further educate yourself on the client's overall lifestyle.

You will want to ask questions about their diet, sleep patterns, leisure interests and any supplements and performance enhancers they are taking. I have found that an increasing number of people are caffeine dependent. Many due to lack of rest. It's a good idea to add a question about caffeine intake to your interview questions. In addition, collecting data about the client's dietary habits is essential. I always have my clients record three days of complete dietary activity and hand it to me for evaluation. This way I can drill down on their habits and calculate the amount of calories they are taking in. I also ask them for a list of their "must have" foods and any foods they are allergic to or simply don't like. All of this is done so that along the way you can make modifications and suggestions to your client's diet that will improve their health and performance.

Another important thing to find out is their work schedule and the tasks they perform on a regular basis at work. Daily activities affect how we feel and perform so it's important to gain a full understanding of how your client lives in order to offer the best advice and prescribe the most effective fitness programming.

Upon completing the PAR-Q, the physical assessment is your next step in the preliminary evaluation phase. The assessment should be formatted in a manner that will allow you to test your client's abilities without injuring them. This test should incorporate all joints and major muscle groups. You will want to evaluate the client's heart rate, strength, stamina, and flexibility, range of motion, balance and overall execution of movement.

All of these are areas you will likely be helping your client improve over the course of your training relationship. Conducting a thorough evaluation in the very beginning allows you to set solid benchmarks and accurately gauge future progresses.

"Age is no barrier. It's a limitation you put on your mind."
- *Jackie Joyner-Kersee*

Give It To Me Straight

Some Trainers focus on making money. Some focus on creating a legacy of successful clients. Then there are those who try to do both. If you can accomplish both, while applying all the principles of accountability and ethics, you have done well. You can use your success stories and bank ledger to gauge how you've done, but there is another way that trumps all of that...the client and community survey.

Wise Trainers understand the necessity for open communication with their clients. If you want to know if you're doing a good Job, ask your clients. Although you may have helped your client make some accomplishments, perhaps they were unhappy with your language, choice of exercises or other things along the way. Having this open dialogue on a daily basis is vital to your attrition rate and credibility with your client. My suggestion is to recap each session. Discuss why you chose the exercises you did, what you observed in your client's performance and what you both need to prepare for in upcoming sessions. Upon offering this recap, ask your client for their feedback.

This is a great opportunity for them to share if they are demotivated or anything else that may inhibit them from making the most of their relationship with you. If you do this, you will have the necessary information to keep your sessions productive and enjoyable.

In conjunction with this Trainer-client communication, it may be a good idea to survey your community to find out what the word on the street is about you. The best way to do this is to ask clients and friends what people are saying. Clients who seek you out have likely heard of you from someone else. That's a great indication of what's being said about you. If your reputation is good, strive to make it great and keep it there.

"You're never a loser until you quit trying."
- *Mike Ditka*

The middle man

When most people fail to close the deal they feel they have lost. Not me. Neither should you. For every door that closes, another one opens. Here's how you can get the door closer to actually open the other door for you.

Let's say you just finished getting the big let down from a prospective client. What do you do next? You do the same thing you would if you had converted them. You tell them how thrilled you are to have met them, and you let them know you will still be a motivational part of their lives. Next, you follow through on what you said. When you see them, show enthusiasm and support. Chat with them about their life and well-being. When you don't see them, add them to your follow up log. Show an interest in them. You are doing all of this because you're a professional and you take a sincere interest in others' quality of life. If you don't have an interest in other people's quality of life, you have no business in our industry. Period.

Here is where something amazing is about to happen. You have spent a lot of time with all of your non-client contacts and they appreciate your concern.

In fact they appreciate you so much that they start telling all their friends about you and how great you are. They are not your clients, yet you treat them with almost as much care as if they were. All of a sudden their friends start calling you. They are already sold because they have already heard how great you are. How easy is that? Zero marketing dollars. Zero selling. The middleman has come through for you. If you're bold enough, you could even reward the middle man with some complimentary sessions and motivate them to promote you even more.

Obviously this is an invaluable relationship, not to be taken lightly. Since you will be in front of plenty of people throughout the month, doesn't it make perfect sense to make each one of those meetings beneficial to all parties? Use this strategy to your advantage. It brings a whole new perspective to a seemingly failed conversion attempt doesn't it?

"You miss 100 percent of the shots you don't take."
- *Wayne Gretzky*

See you at 5

One of the most commonly seen mistakes that Trainers make, is failing to confirm appointments in a timeframe close to the session. Just like us, many of our clients lead busy and sometimes unorganized lives. They need to be reminded where they are supposed to be and when. An appointment confirmation adds an extra layer of accountability. It allows for prompt notice of any needed cancellations or reschedules and it acts as a courtesy as well.

Always confirm appointments and enforce your cancellation policy. You are part of the healthcare system and should receive the same respect and courtesy as the doctor does. A late cancel or no-show at the doctor's office will cost you the same in co-pay as if you did show. This is the penalty for inconveniencing them and not giving them enough notice to possibly accommodate another paying client in your abandoned slot. It's your client's responsibility to honor your policy and it's your courtesy to inform them of it ahead of time. Laying all expectations out there up front will help you avoid awkward conversations and penalty assessments later.

By the same measure, you are also accountable. You are a professional. There is little room for error on your part.

The client pays you and should be offered the best level of service for what they pay. Also, since you are the accountability factor in their lives, you definitely need to set an appropriate example. If you are tardy or reschedule appointments with inconvenient notice, there's no way you can enforce any regulation above that on your client.

"If you always put limits on everything you do, physical or anything else. It will spread into your work and into your life. There are no limits. There are only plateaus, and you must not stay there, you must go beyond them."
– *Bruce Lee*

Do It, Do It, Do It

Motivation is the primary reason people hire a Trainer. Education is readily available. Websites, magazines, television shows all offer free information. There is always a method to find out how to get an effective workout and choose a healthy nutrition regimen. However, many people lack the motivation and discipline to properly plan their days around these things and actually follow through with the plans they do set. This is why you are so important and will never be obsolete.

All professional athletes have Trainers. Most celebrities have Trainers. These are people with extremely hectic schedules yet they make time to meet with a Trainer and keep themselves achieving goals. Not only that, they humble themselves from the star status they have, to listen to the Trainer critique them and motivate them to improve. So why do so many of our common community people feel they don't need anyone to help them? It doesn't matter. The truth is, a lot of them do. Not all, but a lot.

Great Trainers don't allow their clients to slack off. Your job is to encourage them out of their comfort zone while keeping them out of the overtraining zone.

The assessment you did in the preliminary phase will have given you the needed information to know how to gauge these windows of exertion. With this in mind, you already know what they are capable of, so don't let them play the lazy, stubborn, manipulating "I can't" mind games with you. If you give in to this, they will certainly lose respect for you, they will not achieve the set goals and they will blame you for their failure. Trust me, I've seen it happen to Trainers who lacked what they needed to counter this behavior. You may even have some break down and cry, throw tantrums and storm out of your gym when you critique their lack of discipline to the program they have agreed to work through. You have to stand your ground and let them vent. If they respect you, they will pull themselves together and return with an apology and a can-do attitude. Simply put, give them a challenge, push them through it, and celebrate their successes. You will have many successes to celebrate if you do your job properly.

"As long as a man stands in his own way, everything seems to be in his way."
– *Ralph Waldo Emerson*

Do I have to?

There are some things your client may be completely uncomfortable doing. There are a number of reasons this may occur. You may prescribe a movement they have struggled with in the past, it may be a move that makes them feel like they look silly or it may be that the environment is intimidating. If it's the latter, don't try to boost their comfort and confidence with an open talk about blocking out all the other people around who may see them working out. The time will come later for that. A better approach would be to take them to an area with less possible onlookers or give them exercises that they feel confident performing despite the environment.

If you are dealing with a rebellion against the prescribed exercises in general, if it's a legitimate concern, modify the program. For just about anything you plan into a fitness regimen, there is an alternative that will yield similar or identical results that your client may be more receptive to. It's far better to use your knowledge and judgment to develop modifications and alternatives than to be stubborn and lose a client and tarnish your reputation.

"Positive thinking won't let you do anything but it will let you do everything better than negative thinking will."
– *Zig Ziglar*

0 to 100

Nobody gets to his or her personal fitness goal overnight. Although many try to start out going at it with all their might. You'll see them on an elliptical with their eyes closed, cringing and breathing heavily with that look of focused determination. Kind of like what an Olympic runner looks like approaching the finish line.

As a Trainer, it's your job to teach them about periodization and progressive results. As discussed earlier, Body fat percentage, body weight and photograph tracking are essential.

In order to most effectively monitor success, you have to record your findings each session. Preplan your workouts and track your Client's reps per set and poundage as they go. This is especially if they fail to perform the number of preplanned reps. This will add another area of improvement and motivate the client to conquer these small, on the way goals. Some of your movements should be time based. For example, have your client do as many properly executed push-ups as they can in one minute.

Automatically, once they hear the final accomplished number, they will mentally set their own next goal. You didn't have to say anything. It's automatic. With timed exercises, clients almost always strive to beat their last time. Use this method to yours and your client's advantage.

"Believe in yourself! Have faith in your abilities! Without a humble but reasonable confidence in your own powers you cannot be successful or happy."
- *Norman Peale*

One Size Fits All. No It Doesn't.

For most Trainers, programming is the most exciting part of the job. Taking the client out on the floor and "pounding" them is an adrenaline booster like no other. This driving force could also be the death of your business as a Trainer…literally.

As a Trainer, it's extremely important that you listen well in your PAR-Q interview and be attentive in the assessment. Most of the information you need to design your client's program will be learned in these two preliminary meetings. If you do your job well, you will be able to move on in the process of designing a specialized program that specifically fits your client's goals and abilities. Creating this custom fitted program is essential to the success of you both and should never be taken lightly. What you put into this preparatory phase will surely dictate the result that comes out of it.

During the planning phase of programming your client's workouts, be sure to employ movements that are not only effective, but safe for each individual to perform as well.

You want to keep your client out of harms way, but he or she has strengths in some areas so you want to be advantageous at the same time.

Make use of their strengths. This will boost their confidence and maybe increase motivation. You definitely want to work with them on their weaknesses, but educate them on why they have the weaknesses and how together, you will overcome them. Upon doing this, lead them into movements that will fit that plan and explain along the way the reason for each movement. A client who understands your methods will be far more immersed in the client/trainer relationship and will respect you tremendously.

With that in mind, you as an expert will have to assist your client in setting realistic short and long-term goals. A person who has been instructed by their physician to keep their heart rate low and only engage in low impact activity, is not likely to lose 8 pounds in 30 days as a result of exercise. This is an aggressive plan that will require intense activity.

Obviously not the right fit for this client. Knowing how to construct the proper exercise regimen for varying situations is imperative for a Trainer who plans to have a long successful career, free of lawsuits and a bad reputation.

"Strength and growth come only through continuous effort and struggle."
- *Napoleon Hill*

Here We Go Again

When your client says, unenthusiastically, "I know what we're doing today," you need to seriously consider making some changes to your programming. When your client can say with confidence that they know the whole sequence of events about to take place and how it's going to be laid out, you need to act fast to change their perception. Repetitive workouts are boring and can make a person more susceptible to injury through overuse of a particular group of joints, tissue and ligaments. This is harmful on many levels of course. This will demotivate your client, have them quit on you and ruin your reputation as a Trainer. It doesn't stop with you though. Your errors can have an impact on the perception of Personal Trainers in general, so remember, you represent an entire industry. So do your best for the team!

Do whatever you usually do to get in your zone and start creating programs that allow you to put your education and creativity to work. You did your studies, earned your certification and paid a substantial amount of money for those books.

Dig them out, reenergize the scientific sports technician within yourself and start building some kick-butt workouts!

Use the knowledge you have gained in study and in application and start building great programs that will keep your clients engaged, excited and progressing. This is how you build a strong, impressive portfolio and have your clients singing your praises all over town and on the Internet.

"The attitude is very important. Because, your behavior radiates how you feel."
- *Lou Ferrigno*

The More The Merrier

As you recruit new clients and renew existing ones, you will sometimes find the opportunity to form small group training in lieu of one-on-one session. This is particularly beneficial for couples and friends with common goals and abilities. This may also be a good format for existing clients who want to change up things from their normal routine and add some new excitement to their regimen.

Working with couples and groups can be very beneficial for all involved. For you as the Trainer, you make more money per session, build a stronger portfolio by having numerous clients and you learn to manage multiple people at once, which strengthens your communication and leadership skills. For your clients, it adds another angle of accountability. Being part of a team saves them money by splitting the cost of sessions with the group and provides a bit of competitiveness, which boosts performance and progress. There are more benefits on both sides, but these are the primary ones.

As the professional, you have to spot the opportunity to form these groups. Once you are seasoned in your craft, it's pretty simple to pinpoint when it's best to use this method of training and for whom.

Look for cues in the initial assessment and PAR-Q interview. You may pick up on things about your interviewee like "former athlete," "Need to be pushed" and "competitive". Attributes like these are common among those who enjoy small group training. They can compete against and motivate the others in the group and they are often excited by the overall progress of the whole team.

"Hard work and training. There's no secret formula. I lift heavy, work hard and aim to be the best."
- *Ronnie Coleman*

So How Are Things Going?

Throughout your career as a Personal Trainer, you will meet tons of people whom you hope to make your clients. Unfortunately, no matter how good you are at selling your services and motivating people, you will not land them all. That's not always a bad thing. I'll explain why, but first I have to stress the importance of making a stellar first impression. If people have a positive remembrance of a first meet and subsequent encounters with you, it will be far easier to have them open up to you about their struggles of trying to make accomplishments on their own. Plus it will assist the possibility of them having thoughts of considering asking you for your help along the way.

Follow up with past clients and prospects that originally turned you down. They may be failing, and if they are, they will be thrilled you reached out to them. These will often be your best clients and spokespeople. The reason is likely because you came to the rescue when things were going down hill for them.

This is where you can turn a negative (no-sale) into a positive turnaround. This will always be their impression of you and they will be forever grateful as long as you get them to a place they can feel good about themselves and see significant progress.

"We can be tired, weary and emotionally distraught, but after spending time alone with God, we find that He injects into our bodies energy, power and strength."
- *Charles Stanley*

Conclusion

So here's the deal. Personal Trainers are necessary. We will never be obsolete no matter how many fat burner pills; fad diets or exercise machines are released. We motivate people to go to heights they dream of but can't reach on their own. We contribute to strong, healthy and productive communities. We help people combat illness and reclaim vitality. We are the essential element. Personal training is an art form. Become a master.

www.ingramcontent.com/pod-product-compliance
Lightning Source LLC
Chambersburg PA
CBHW071323040426
42444CB00009B/2069